How

Compulsive

Lying

Step-By-Step Strategies to Quit the Habit of Lying

David Joseph

Copyright © 2018 David O.J

ISBN: 9781790370825

Dedication

This book is dedicated to my wife, Debbie, and all those who love the truth.

Table of Contents

When we decide to lie, we privilege some other value over honesty. In an attempt to conceal the truth from other people, we hide our true identity. People will see us differently and possibly give us overly positive feedback about our abilities. Lying can bring instant gratification and appears easy part to shy away from reality at the moment but inevitably makes life more complicated. It may cover the shame and the guilt for the moment, but will not render a realistic solution to the problem. We may gain an advantage or avoid confrontation in the short-term, but when we are caught we jeopardize the effectiveness of our communication and the strength of our relationships.

Over time, the deception can eat away at our self-esteem; undermining our fundamental sense of dignity and worthiness.

This book is an ultimate guide that introduces you to the world of lying. The main goal is to ensure that you have a clear understanding of how the self-indulgent habit of lying actually affects your life negatively. The book shares what causes compulsive lying, why people lie in the first place, as well as what happens when an urge to lie comes up. It contains a step-by-step strategy that will help you break away from the habit and help you take control of your life.

1 Introduction

Lying and deception are common human behaviors which always generate serious consequences. We often give in to lying because it appears the easiest way to walk through a difficult situation successfully. Lying provides flexibility for mutual interactions and easy self expression. According to research carried out at the University of Virginia, an average person lies at least once or twice a day. The results further show that we tend to tell the most lies to the people we love, an action which eventually render the relationship less significant. It can sometimes be normal for people to feel constrained to lie because they want to hide their true feelings or be secretive about certain facets of their life. Some of these lies are little white lies intended to care for someone else's feelings. Some can be much more serious (like embellishing our credentials) or even sinister (covering up a crime). Whatever the motive, lying is ethically wrong and is always discouraged. But, unfortunately it is quite commonplace nowadays and comes to us naturally.

Lying often begins as a means of gaining attention, boost self-esteem, or to increase social standing. It can be fun at first and brings immediate gratification but over time you will see the need to stop lying as the benefits can't stand the test of time. Liars often find that they have burnt many bridges and hurt themselves in many ways. Soon when people realize that you lie about everything, they may begin to create some distances and isolate you. The problem can easily affect your social life, career, and business.

Lying influences the sort of choices you make on a daily basis which affects your happiness as a whole. Constant lying usually results in others not taking you seriously as an individual. Once people have realized that you are a liar, gaining their confidence becomes difficult. People may believe your imaginative lies and treat you for whom you say you are instead of who you really are as a person. Your personality may remain imperceptible and if care is not taken, forgotten. This brings about the necessity to stop lying so that you can redeem your reputation, rebuild your credibility and regain your confidence.

People that lie impulsively often have many other issues that are related. Lying is among the common causes of mental stress. As long you are willing to admit that you need help and can recognize your lying habit, you can take steps to improve your condition. Addressing the root causes of your lying and receiving therapy and medication for the personality disorder can help you to overcome the bad habit. When we are caught lying directly or seen lying to someone else, we lose a measure of credibility and trust from those around us. Ultimately, deceitful habits are shortsighted. We may gain an advantage or avoid confrontation in the short-term, but when we are caught, we jeopardize the effectiveness of our communication and the strength of our relationships. Trust and credibility are easy to lose, but they are incredibly difficult to earn back.

Lying is a fundamental part of the conventional work process and determines a lot on how we are being perceived around business associates, friends, and even family members.

Telling the truth will decrease the lying induced stress that you are under. It is strenuous and time-consuming trying to remember what lies you have told and to whom. You will realize that it is a great relief, to tell the truth.

Deception causes unhappiness due to the feeling of guilt resulting from living a fake life. You are always under tension due to the need to protect your lies and the provision of actual creative ways to stay above the truth. Truth has been reputed to boost self-esteem, enhance insightfulness and reduce social anxiety and depression. When you master honesty, you can view things in clear perspective without delusions. Your circumstances begin to improve and you will develop closer friendships with high quality people. You will be admired and seen as someone who is respectable and honorable when you consistently act with honor and integrity. You will become free from the limitations the habit of dishonesty had imposed on your life.

2 Reasons for Lying

There are wide ranges of reasons why people tell lies. Some indulge in the habit to cover up and look better in front of others. Some are afraid of the consequences of speaking the truth hence they resolve to deception to pass through a difficult situation and maintain good relationships. No matter what the reason, lying is a complex phenomenon to fall into. Some people get so accustomed to lying that they do so even when it is unnecessary.

Understanding the reason people lie can help you get relief from the pain. Awareness of the deeply entrenched social conditioning that influences a person to lie will help you drop your misplaced expectations of a liar. Managing your expectations will go a long way to dissolving your emotional reactions to their conditioned behavior.

When people first discover how lying works, they lack the moral understanding of when quit the habit. Lying can bring instant gratification and appears easy part to shy away from reality at the moment, but inevitably makes life more complicated.

The variety of reasons people lie include

• To hide true feelings or compensate for the reality

• To manipulate or maintain a sense of power over others or a situation

- Need for approval or wanting to please others

- A feeling of superiority over others

- Protecting someone or themselves

- Avoiding punishment and self-protection

- To gain Sympathy of others

- To impress others and cause a better impression

- Avoid hurting people's feelings

A sociopath

A sociopath is someone who lies continually to get his way and does so without consideration for others. Sociopaths are often amiable and charismatic, but they use their talented social skills for selfish reasons.

Also, they are self-centered individuals with little or no regard for the rights and feelings of others.

Compulsive liars

We can define a compulsive liar as someone who lies out of habit. They will resort to telling lies, regardless of the situation. Lying is their usual and impulsive way of responding to questions. Most people that lie do so for certain reasons and will select what to lie about, but a habitual liar, on the other hand, will lie uncontrollably for no clear reason.

Telling the truth is awkward and telling lies is routine. They bend the truth about everything (large and small). Compulsive lying is thought to develop in early childhood, due to being raised in an environment where lying was seen as a way of life.

Most compulsive liars seem to live in a fantasy world deliberately designed by themselves. The very fact that their lie could be found out is insignificant to them. They seem to have developed strong hurdle to commonsense thinking and a guilty conscience.

Beyond occasional patterns of lying, compulsive lying is often a symptom of a much larger personality disorder. A persistent cycle of lying can point to other mental issues like pathological lying or related problems such as sociopathy. Pathological lying is a long history of frequent and repeated lying for which no apparent psychological motive or external benefit can be discerned. There are a variety of personality and behavioral disorders that are related to pathological lying, some are narcissistic personality disorder and borderline personality disorder. Pathological liars choose to lie because they have a compulsive need to cover up their true self. They may lie to make themselves appear smarter or more superior than others so that they can hide their weakness. Their lying habit always has internal motives rather than an external reason. The more often they lie the more it affects their career, their relationships, and their family. Compulsive lying not adequately addressed can easily ruin a relationship. It is hard for the person involved to see, but it hurts those who are around it.

3 How Lying Destroys a Relationship

Lying is one of the quickest ways to ruin a beautiful relationship. It is a widespread problem with many people nowadays affecting their happiness and choices. A relationship needs trust to thrive continuously. Trust is a vital ingredient in building a solid relationship. Deceit can be one of the quickest ways to strip that needed trust from a relationship. When trust is lost in a relationship it gives way for distrust and misunderstanding.

You can't constantly lie and expect to gain people's confidence. Lying is a slow killer of relationship.

Here are some of the many ways in which lying affects relationships of all kinds.

Lies Erode Trust

Lies and trust cannot easily coexist; lies erode trust and without trust, there's no relationship. When we lie, we are erecting a wall between us and the person we are lying to. Because lie will only bring a temporary relief, it can never solve a problem permanently. The foundation for a strong and successful relationship is built on trust. When this is lost, the chances of a total collapse are very high. Lies can utterly damage the foundation of a relationship and make it unbefitting for one or both parties. It can be devastating and painful to discover that the one we loved and trust has betrayed us. It can shatter the confidence we have in our partner. Once you uncover a lie for the first time, you become suspicious of the person.

Your interaction suffers, and doubts begin to replace trust that once exists in the relationship. You begin to live in expectation of future untruths from that person. Once trust is broken, it's extremely hard to rebuild. *When you tell a lie once your truth becomes questionable.*

Lying Shows a Lack of Respect

When you are lied to, you feel cheated and disrespected. It proves that the other person does not place a significant value upon the relationship. Being told the truth confers the feeling of respect upon the recipient and proves that the other person is not prepared to jeopardize the relationship by deceiving them. Lying shows a lack of respect and distrust. As soon as lack of respect manifests in a relationship, it begins to put great strain on all aspects of the relationship and, if left unchecked, it can damage the relationship.

Lying Demonstrates Selfishness

Lies can also be an indication of selfishness and disregard for the other party. When you lie, you are basically putting your self-interest above others. A successful relationship thrives on mutual understanding and tolerance for each other. Unwillingness to make a sacrifice for the greater, long-term good of a relationship put strains on a relationship. Self-centeredness makes the other party feel unimportant in the relationship which can lead to less commitment and eventually the collapse of such relationship.

Lies can Permeate the Other Aspects of Your Life Without You Even Knowing it

No one tells just one lie, when in you lie in your personal life, it doesn't end there. Lies can transcend other aspects of your life without you even knowing it. Lies not only grow but they can become addictive especially if you have gotten away with a few already. There is a tendency to want to lie every time you find yourself in a sticky situation because lie seems the easier way to get out. The fact of the matter is that when you lie and gets away with it, you become invincible and so you are more likely to want to lie even more. Before you know it lies begin to manifest in all aspects of your life. You begin to lie on the job, in the social circles, and among friends.

Feeling a Fool for Believing a Lie

The moment the victim of a lie realizes he has been lied to he becomes upset, feeling being fooled forever falling for the lies. His perception of the partner will be perpetually changed by the agony of the deceit. The ugly experience may erode all the positive feelings he\she may have towards the partner. The hurt may open up a crack in the relationship and destroy any sense of cohesiveness that once existed in the relationship. The affected person may feel cheated and maltreated and spend all his time planning to hit back and revenge.

Lies Create a Sense of Imbalanced

For a relationship to work and stand the test of time it requires commitment from both parties. There should be a balance of effort from both parties; they must give equal commitment and energy to it. This balance creates the feeling of trust and understanding that strengthened a relationship. It will bring the best out in each other and raise the confidence level. Lying upset the flow of this natural equilibrium and causes the scales to tilt towards one side. For the person on the receiving end of a lie, the experience can be devastating and make them feel as though they have put their heart and soul on the line, only to be disappointed by a deceptive partner.

The Liars are Conning Themselves too

Lie perpetrators are being untruthful to themselves. When we decide to lie, we privilege some other value over honesty. In an attempt to conceal the truth from other people, we hide our true identity. People will see us differently and possibly give us overly positive feedback about our abilities. Any relationship built on this hypocritical approach to life cannot stand the test of time. Over time, we will lose the confidence of people when the truth unfolds.

One Lie Often Leads to Another

A lie cannot stand alone. Lie breeds lie, attempt to defend a lie and make it real often leads to another. Before you know it, lying will soon become the norm of the relationship. Where lying becomes routine, the relationship suffers. Any foundation built on deceit will eventually give way to reality.

Feeling of guilt

The deceiver feels guilty, or at least uncomfortable, during intimate moments with the deceived person. He tends to avoid certain topics with the deceived person due to the feeling of guilt. A guilty conscience needs no accuser. When we violate our conscience by hiding the truth,

23

we experience anxiety generated by guilt. Over time, the deception can eat away at our self-esteem; undermining our fundamental sense of dignity and worthiness.

Dishonesty prevents real intimacy with a partner.

Intimacy is based on trust and genuineness. It is the ability to be vulnerable not only physically, but also emotionally. When we are open and honest, it makes our partner see our flaws. When our worst shame is laid bare and our partner accepts it and accepts us in spite of the shortcomings, then we can breathe a sigh of relief. We can relax and be ourselves. Having a loving partner who accepts as we are can help ease any stress.

That is what intimacy is all about. On the other hand, lying gives the perpetrator a false sense of security in the relationship.

4 How to Tell if Someone is Lying

Behavioral differences between honest and lying persons are sometimes difficult to differentiate and measure. But, when it comes to detecting lies, there are some subtle physical and behavioral signs that reveal deception to watch for. Understanding these indicators is crucial for self-awareness to develop the ability to effectively deal with compulsive liars. In addition, you will be able to regulate your time with things and people that do not matter and offers little benefits.

Body language can be a useful tool in the detection of lies; some of the most common signs include shifty eyes, constant fidgeting, and avoiding eye contact.

Being vague and non-committal: If the speaker seems to offer few details - intentionally leaving out important facts in the story. If you observe that the speaker is not confident and refuses to really pin down his story and consistently giving you unclear answers that could get him off the hook more easily. You should begin to doubt the person. Most times, they will try as much as possible to avoid issues.

They know the significance of speaking less when conveying their lies. Back in the days, lying is usually detected when someone speaks too much or keeps explaining one incident over and over. The excessive explanations or words are red flags even a savvy can indicate in a liar. So the most defensive strategy is to say as little as possible.

Over thinking: If the individual seems to be thinking too hard to fill in the details of the story, struggling to provide specific details when a story is challenged it might be because they are deceiving you.

A Person Proclaims His Honesty Repeatedly

To lend credence to their stories, liars often use phrases emphasizing the legitimacy of their stories. Their statements are often characterized with phrases such as "to speak the truth" "I was brought up to never lie," "to be perfectly honest." "God is my witness." "As you know I can't tell you lie". When you are speaking in a plain language all these are not necessary. Truth can stand on its own without being supported by any evidence.

Inconsistency

Liars can't keep their stories straight. When you ask a lying person to repeat his story over again, you will probably notice inconsistency and cracks in the story. In the process of repeating the made-up story, the liar is likely to say something contradictory or outright false. It's difficult to keep track of information that isn't truthful. Although there might be reasons for changing stories, even when you ask honest people to retell a story there can be changes. Because, he may remember additional details which can make the story to differ slightly with their earlier presentation, but there will be no contradiction or inconsistency in the story. But a liar explanation is often characterized by inconsistency and loopholes. Usually, they fail to remember details upon retelling or add new information that contradicts the earlier story. Oftentimes, liars say what comes to their mind to support their claim.

Relating a Story in Reverse Order

Lying is more mentally taxing than telling the truth- it is more cognitively demanding. Liars typically need to exert much more mental energy toward monitoring their behaviors to make their stories credible for people to believe. A good way to catch a liar is to ask him to relate his story in reverse order. When you ask them to relate a story in reverse order you throw them off balance. Studies suggest that increasing the mental workload makes lying more difficult. Even a professional liar can find this task a hard one to tackle effectively as cracks in the story and inconsistency might become obvious.

A Person fidget and Fusses for no Reason

Sometimes liars fidget more than usual during a conversation because they fear being found out. If someone seems unstable and keeps performing a random physical action that appears unnecessary-adjusting his chair frequently, cleaning his glasses excessively, or dusting off the (clean) table in front of him—he may be lying. The guilt makes him nervous and restless.

Questions Repetition

Liars always end up repeating questions before answering them. They do this in an attempt to buy time when asked questions. They repeat the question back to create time strain so that they will have the time to think of the perfect lie. For example, "boy, why did you come home late last night? Instead of answering the question directly-what follows is usually "Why did I come home late last night?" This is an attempt to create time strain to think of the perfect lie that matches the question.

Although most liars often fabricate answers to questions in anticipation of questions, concocting answers may be the best way to lie successfully. But when you fabricate too much similar answers about the same event, you may get confused on the perfect answer to use at the moment.

Anxious About the Listener's Attention

Liars pay too much concern on the listener's reaction and react to every posture even when it is not necessary. They are always anxious and feel like that person is looking through them, and so they will try to justify their fallacy by explaining the more. In some circumstances, the postures of the listener affect their posture and the tone of the conversation as well.

Liars are good at reading people's reaction more than any other person in society. They are good observers, who can easily adapt to any condition to sell their deceit.

The Lack of Specifics

Dishonesty people lack specifics when it comes to the actual conveyance of information. When challenged about the authenticity of the information, an honest person may come up with specific details. But deceptive people often deviate from specifics. Instead of providing more details, they deviate from the specifics by using emotional reactions to get people to believe them. Pathological liars are good at this, and you may not even realize when they do it.

5 Reasons to Stop Lying

Telling the truth will likely radically decrease the stress that you are under. It is strenuous and time-consuming to be conscious of what lies you have told and to whom. You will not be able to remember the lies hence you give a different reason and react differently to the same issue when you have cause to do so. You will find that it is great relief, to tell the truth. *If you tell the truth it becomes a part of your past. If you tell a lie, it becomes a part of your future.*

When you lie, you hurt your mind and make yourself out of touch with reality. You disguise and project deceit and falsehood to the world. When this turns into a habit you lose your sense of personal esteem and become dishonesty. People may not know that you are telling lies but right within, you know the truth because you can only lie to people but not yourself. The guilt of deceit will hang on unless you decide to change and come out clean. If you wish to live with respect and dignity, you have to stop lying and live uprightly.

Abraham Lincoln said: *"If you once forfeit the confidence of your fellow citizens, you can never regain their respect and esteem."*

Here are a few good reasons to stop lying

To connect with others again

Lying to other people deny you the ability to make friends and feel truly part of the community. Good relationships are based on people's ability to interact amicably with others. The more you interact with people, the closer you get. Deciding to stop lying can save your face and help you maintain the dignity that you once enjoyed among your family and friends.

To gain back other people's trust.

When people realize that you lie about everything, they may begin to create some distance, making you alone. They'll protect themselves from further manipulation by no longer placing their trust and confidence in you.

The only way to gain back their confidence is to start being honest and continue being honest until they can see that in you. After a while, they will begin to trust your word again. This could take some years, so it's ideal to start now.

People will not and should not trust you as much as they did before. You have to prove that you can be reliable by following through on your promises. Accept the consequences of telling lies in the past. You're going to pay for your past lies. Be steadfast and live uprightly. Similarly, be willing to suffer the slight, daily consequences of telling the truth. Gradually truth will pay off and you will begin to regain people's confidence.

Lie breaks down trust

Liars usually lose authority and gain the reputation of a hypocrite. Friedrich Nietzsche once said, "I'm upset that you lied to me, I'm upset that from now I cannot believe you."

Heartbreak caused by dishonesty tends to be hard on the victim, especially when he used to have total trust in the person. It is easy to lose authority as a result of your lie, regardless of how small. This becomes worse when the people that once trusted you now label you as a pathological liar. On the other hand, honest people are often appreciated by others around them. The person who speaks the truth in spite of circumstances always gains respect and total authority in his environment. Being trustworthy is a good trait of character that increases your self-confidence.

Less stress

Telling the truth boosts your immunity, reduces depression and sharpens thinking. When you tell the truth, you are less tensed and sad because you don't have to feel anxious about all your white lies. Speaking the truth always gives a feeling of emotional and mental calmness. Lying is among the common causes of mental stress. Deceptiveness breeds sadness due to the feeling of apprehensive caused by telling lies. When you lied, you are always under tension due to the need to protect your lies and the provision of actual creative ways to stay above the truth.

Inner conflicts

When you tell a lie you have to tell more to cover up. And once you reach the limits, mental craziness will set in and you may begin to run away from the lies and places or people you lied to. This usually creates various inner conflicts and stress within you, which can affect your mood and give you more problems. Furthermore, it affects your confidence and self-esteem. The truth will make you free but when you choose the path of lie to accomplish your goals you enslave your conscience. The self-imposed anxiety can create more problems even when you try to fake confidence.

The inner controversy caused by habitual lying can be harmful to your emotional health and overall well-being.

Lying is the signal of a bigger problem

Practicing lying continuously can lead to bigger problems later in life. When you tell lies all the time it turns into a habit. People will begin to be skeptical about you and try to avoid dealing with you. They will be skeptical of the information you share even if it is true. Lying should be dealt with in good time before it turns into compulsive behaviors. Disappointment that comes with lies is often difficult to accommodate by the perpetrator. Some people tell lies to get people's favor and when they don't achieve their aim after waiting endlessly they become chronically stressed.

Limitations in accomplishment

When you mentally create the history of a successful life you want, you may be depriving yourself the opportunity of achieving the desire in reality. If you lie about your success and you label yourself as a successful individual. Your interaction will be directed to avoid opportunities that will provide for such experiences, thus limiting the chance of meeting people who can offer help to discover great ideas for running a fulfilled life. When you make people believe that you don't need help and you are independent, they won't see the need to help you even when you need help. If you give up telling lies by living a true life you will have an opportunity to live a better life.

Lying won't solve problems

According to Tad Williams "We tell lies when we are afraid... afraid of what we don't know, afraid of what others will think, afraid of what will be found out about us. But every time we tell a lie, the thing that we fear grows stronger"

Lying doesn't solve problems. It can only provide instant gratification which will fade away with time. The moment you realize this important fact the good for you to seek to eradicate lies from your life before it wreaks uncontrollable havoc. It may cover the shame and the guilt for the moment, but will not render a realistic solution to the problem. Instead, it can redouble the problems, and make you lose everything-your job family and friends. Remember that honesty is the best policy in any circumstances. Although, it may provoke grief, anger, sadness, and disappointment, but will surely provide the actual path to follow in order to reach a real solution.

When your interpersonal relationship suffers, you become the worse person to look up to when someone is trying to solve a problem.

Liars don't have peace.

Roselyn once commented: "I can say that not lying is a very relaxing way of life." Lying is stressful; you have to worry all the time about remembering old lies or getting in trouble later on when the truth comes out. You're always rehearsing the lies you've told in your head, trying to keep track of what you've told to which person and organize yourself for the next episode. You need to develop a carefully crafted charisma to be on top of the game and ensure that your lies are not found out. When you're truthful, you don't have those worries or the negative consequences of your lies. Truth can stand the test of time.

Lying doesn't work in the long run. Once you are labeled as a liar, you've blown it as rebuilding trust may be impossible. If you have decided that it is time to stop lying, the following steps will help you take back your life.

Figure out why you lie.

Knowing the root cause of your lying is the first step to making the desired change in your life. Some people formed the habit of lying from a very early age. Perhaps you learned as a child that it is not easy to navigate difficult situation until you lie, and you continued the practice as a teenager and beyond. Once you form the pattern of lying, it gradually develops into a habit which refuses to die. It may be difficult, telling the truth again.

Do you lie as a means to make yourself look better, gain attention, boost self-esteem, or to increase social standing. Or you see lying as an easy way to boost your status at work, in your social circle, and even among your loved ones.

Maybe you routinely lie as a way to gain control over situations and make other people do what you want them to do. When you can see an easy path to getting what you want through telling a lie, telling the truth is hard. You need to figure out why you lie to be able to overcome the addiction.

Determine why you want to stop

If you don't have clear reasons for stopping the habit, it's pretty difficult to overcome the practice and become an honest person. You have to think hard about the effect of lying on your personality, relationships, and the course of your life. Think of what you have lost as a result of living a deceptive life. When you thought of the consequences of getting caught you become restless. Some lies may have given you untold hardship and nightmares.

Make a commitment to quit the habit.

Once you are determined to quit the habit, treat it as you would any other addiction and make a serious commitment to quit. The next step is to set a target and get a plan in place. This is going to require a lot of hard work and thoughtfulness but with strong determination, you will win. Be determined to follow through on your promises, soon you will realize that it pays to be honest.

Get outside help.

It is always tough to quit any kind of addiction by yourself. Reach out to people who can provide support and help hold you accountable to achieve your goal. There are people who have been through this and can offer good advice. Talk to the people that are close to you that can offer help. There are some people in your life who will want to help you stop lying, even if they've been a victim of your deceit. Tell them about your plan to quit the habit so they can provide some support. Also, you will be able to gain their confidence if they know you are sincere with your resolution and notice positive changes in your life.

Work with a therapist

It is crucial that you work with a therapist that you feel comfortable with and can be honest with. Most therapy sessions will revolve around behavior modification. It is essential to determining the underline factor of your behavior as well as understanding what effect your lying has on your relationship. Work with your therapist to figure your emotional needs and to find ways to honestly meet all these needs without resorting to telling lies. You may take part in role-playing exercises with your therapist to help you deal with situations that would normally result in you telling a lie. It is imperative to make him aware of any setbacks you may experience so that you can work through them. You may discover that you have underlying psychological issues that must be dealt with while working with your therapist. If he feels that medication will help your situation, you may be referred to a physician.

Identify your triggers.

It is good to identify the triggers that cause you to avoid telling the truth if you want to successfully stop lying. Identifying the situations, emotions, people, or places that tend to cause you to lie will help you to avoid the trigger or find a way to handle it differently. When you know the underlying factor you can confront it effectively with honesty. Think of your lying pattern and analyze why you lie and why telling the truth can ultimately help you. As you determine to develop the habit of telling the truth, the patterns in your thinking that compel you to lies will become more obvious. It's important to stay aware of the pattern so that you won't slip back into the habit of lying.

If you can't say something true, don't say anything at all. When you're confronted with a trigger and under temptation to lie, it will be proper to refrain from speaking at all. You are not under obligation to answer questions you don't want to answer or talk when you don't feel to do so.

Pay attention to the physical symptoms that signify you are about to lie. Avoid situations that have typically made you feel you have to say something untrue. If you are asked a question you don't feel you can answer truthfully, it will be good to avoid answering the question rather than telling lies.

Practice actively telling the truth.

When you practice telling the truth, the more you tell the truth, the easier it will become for you. At a certain point, telling the truth will put you in the type of situation you've always deceitfully evade but you should be resolute. To strengthen your determination you should learn how to face consequences. Facing the unpleasant consequences is better than lying because it reinforces your character and help builds trust with other people.

Let truth, rather than lies becomes your habitual reaction when you're confronted with the trials of life. If you've lied a lot to people, it may take a while before they believe and take you seriously. You have to work on building trust with them. Make honesty the core of your character. Honesty is a quality that is honed through the hard work of being strong in difficult situations. It is a character trait that is highly cherished across cultures and societies all over the world. Everyone fails to be honest at times, but honorable people pick themselves up keep trying to do the right thing with every difficult prevailing circumstance.

The more you tell the truth and meet the expectations of other people, the more you build sound relationships with people. The good relationship brings trust, and banishes loneliness which creates community.

7 How to Stop Lying in a Relationship

In a relationship, most people believe lying is better than the truth because lying is more comfortable and pleasant to the ear. But the truth is every time you lie, you create a crack in the wall of a relationship because lying is a temporary solution to a permanent problem. Telling the truth and making someone cry is better than telling a lie and making someone smile. Truth builds your relationship, while lying can shatter everything you've built for years. An ideal relationship is built on mutual trust, sincerity, respect and personal freedom.

Lies can hurt other people and destroy a relationship when all the truths are showed off. Here are some ways and tips on how to stop lying in a relationship.

Do not mix the truth

Be honest in all your conversation and do not compromise by mixing the truth with lies. If an issue is half pleasant and half unpleasant give the full details. In an attempt to make the story palatable, do not present the pleasant and leave out the other. You can present your story by starting with the more pleasant part of the story and ending with the less pleasant.

A true relationship is when you can tell each other anything and everything. No secrets and no lies.

Do not compromise in any way by adding, removing or integrating the truth with falsehood. Honesty, regardless of how bad it tastes, is a crucial factor that determines the strength of your intimacy. Someone has said that telling the truth and making someone cry is better than telling a lie and making someone smile.

Backtrack immediately you lie

During a conversation, when you realize that you just added an element of a lie, backtrack immediately, and tell the real truth. Admit your mistake and apologize. This action is one of the quickest ways you can use to rebuild trust. Your admittance will give your partner a new perception about you. It will help you start rebuilding the process of getting people more comfortable with you again step by step.

Noticing that you attempted to say something pleasant in order to avoid hurting them and then realizing the truth is the best, makes you a better person.

You don't need to tell your partner that you have just lied simply saying sorry and replace the lie with the real truth will redeem the situation.

Even when anger is triggered, you should be able to calm the person down instead of creating excuses to justify your mistakes. The anger will pass if they understand your honest and your problems.

Note your lies

You should get a notebook that you can carry all the time to note your lies. On the notebook, indicate the days you deceive people the most and the relating triggers. Use a week or two monitoring the occurrence of your lies and make sure you keep track of each occurrence. On the notebook, write down all the events that lead to lying. What advantage you gain by using deceit and what would have happened if you confront the matter honestly. You should also Include in the note your feelings or emotions before lying and after lying.

It is equally important to, keep track of your honesty in order to find out your motivations and in what circumstance you feel comfortable being honest. After about a week of writing about such feelings, you can create time to analyze the situation. By this way, you will remember to fix your lie and never do it again.

Choose the right time for the hurtful truth

You should choose a good time to present the hurtful truth. If you feel your partner can be upset by telling the truth you can carefully look for a time when you think they might be ready. If you think you cannot answer a question truthfully at a particular moment, you should politely ask them to give you time and reorganize yourself. This is not an attempt to buy time to cook another story but to help you decide the right time to talk to your partner about something sensitive and to also find a way to say it in a pleasant way.

Admit your problems

The first important step is to admit you have problems and then actualize on the reason you always need to lie. It is common to wish to justify yourself that you are not wrong when you are lying. Stop convincing yourself that you are always right and your way is the best.

You need to confess to your partner the reasons you lie. It might be because you want him to be proud of you or maybe you don't want him to be disappointed in your weaknesses. Admitting and open up to your spouse about your problem will create an opportunity for both of you to work towards creating an enduring change. You will realize that there is no need to look completely perfect for your partner.

A relationship thrives when strengths, weaknesses, and flaws are showcased without the fear of being judged or scorned. Struggling together to achieve a common goal in your relationship is crucial in achieving a greater intimacy and trust. If you cannot struggle to grow together, you will always grow apart. You may not have enough power to put the situation under control, but with the support of the significant other, you could take the bull by the horn and create a better life.

Think before you speak

Take time to think deeply about what you are going to say. This is the best way to help you gain control of the bad habit. It helps you to evaluate the consequences of your words and its effects on your partner.

It is said that words can either be a nurturer or cause the death of a relationship. Once words leave your mouth, they are like an arrow that cannot be withdrawn. You might have said some things in your life that you would like to take back but alas! It is impossible. You just cannot undo the damage of anger and the resultant effects of uncontrolled words. Whenever you feel the urge to tell lies, just be quiet and resort to active listening. Active listening is a mind control technique that helps in keeping negative thoughts under control.

Find Out What Pressured You to Lie

You need to analyze the cause of your habit of constant lying before you can successfully pull yourself out of the mess. You need to ask yourself, what am I trying to hide? What would have been a better way, to tell the truth?

You will realize that lying is never worth all the sufferings that you have to go through. Lies can never do any good either to you or the person you lied to. It takes a lot of truth to gain trust, but just one lie to lose it all.

The feeling of insecurities, and hopelessness that motivate you to lie might be actually a result of nothingness. If you think your partner is trying to leave you, confront them and try to find out what they feel and whether they are under pressure in the relationship. Make yourself attractive to them by developing your personal abilities. Physical, mental and career improvement is necessary to develop an attractive personality, capable of maintaining a relationship for a long time.

A lie is a threat to any type of relationship, whether it's a friendship or a romance. Lie erodes trust and can make things hard to get back on track. Trust is the foundation of a good relationship. It is the fundamental process of love and intimacy. A relationship without trust is characterized by anger, insecurity, anxiety, fear, and disrespect; it brings suspicion, and asking needless questions. Once it trust is lost in a relationship, it is usually hard to put back together again. Therefore, maintaining trust is essential to having satisfying relationships. If you have lied to someone, or you fall victim, there are some steps to take to fix it. Both of you must want to work at rebuilding the lost trust.

Rebuilding a Relationship after Lying: If You Are the Liar

Accepting responsibilities

If you want to rebuild a relationship after lying, the first step always has to be taking some responsibility. You have to admit that you lied to someone. Confess and come clean about the full extent of your dishonesty. Don't make confession halfway expecting things will be alright. Avoid covering up or hiding further details to prevent falling into another lie. Take some responsibility rather than making excuses, remind yourself what happened and admit your fault. This stage is important because you need to be at peace with yourself before making peace with the people you have deceived. When you admit your guilt you should expect an emotional outburst from the other person. No matter what emotion they show, treat it respectfully. Remember, you are responsible for this problem; the best way to rebuild and move on is by opening up. Plan how to step forward and admit your mistake. It might be humiliating, but that may be the price you have to pay for your past dishonesty. Every act of dishonesty has a price.

Be ready to apologize

The next step towards genuine reconciliation is to tender a sincere apology. If you are actually remorseful for what you did, you need to apologize properly. If you have lied to someone for whatever reason and you want proper reconciliation, they deserve to receive a meaningful apology.

Let your partner know that you regret your action and promise never to do it again. Say it with feeling and all sincerity. Don't make an empty promise. Apologizing and not meaning it will be unfair to your partner, and also to yourself. Prove that you can be reliable by following through on your promises and be willing to keep to your word. You need to show your readiness and commitment to doing right again, even if it's difficult for you. When apologizing, accept responsibility and avoid justifying your actions. Let the person you betrayed know that it comes from the bottom of your heart. If they know that you are remorseful they are more likely to forgive you. Have it in mind that people will not and should not trust you as much as they did before. You have to prove that you can be reliable by following through on your promises. Accept the consequences of telling lies in the past and convince your partner of your genuineness.

Be honest

Be truthful about whatever you lied about; make sure you're honest about it. You have to reveal the whole truth to the victim of your dishonesty so that he\she can assess the situation and react accordingly. Giving the full picture of what actually transpired is critical this time; it will allow your partner to make their own judgments rather than being influenced wrongly by your opinion. Keeping things will not help in this matter; it will only make you look worse when the truth eventually comes out. Your action has already caused considerable damages, so it better to get it all out of your system so you can begin to heal the wounds and move on.

Allow the person you lied to time to reflect

Depending on the severity of your betrayer, it can take a long time to get over and forgive. You have to realize that you can't determine the effect of your action on the victim of your lie. It can cut deeper than you intend. Therefore you have to wait and allow him time to forgive you, rebuilding trust takes time. Stay patient, but be persistent in your own efforts. You don't have power over this but you can only influence the outcome. It is not mainly about your feelings. You owe them the time to assess their feelings – you upset them, and they don't owe you anything back. When he forgives, be prepared to rebuild the strained relationship, or risk the trust slipping away from you yet again. Work to be a better person in order to gain what you lost due to your previous actions.

Learn from your mistakes and make sure you don't do anything to hurt them again. Begin to do things perfectly now and don't allow your past to catch up with you again and lead you astray. Understand that things may never be quite the same after the nasty experience, but if you show that you are now a trustworthy person, some level of trust can usually be restored.

How to Rebuild a Relationship after Lying: If Someone Lied to You

Accept the reality

Be open and come to terms with what happened whenever the other person has shown an effort to make amends for the action. Be prepared to rebuild the damaged relationship. Accept that you've been lied to and prepare to move on. Getting all the anger and disappointment out of the way clears your mind and free you from prejudice and hatred. The angrier you are, the less receptive you are to what the other party has to say. There must be a sincere and genuine effort to work out the issues.

Consider the apology

You should be welcoming to a person who is trying to correct his mistakes. A person who is ready to apologize for wrongdoings without being cruel or defensive is usually genuine. Listening to the apology is the bigger thing to do; this will give you a sense of how genuine they are and prevent you from making the wrong decision.

Express yourself

Express yourself honestly, talk about what you have suffered as a result of the incident. This is important to make the other party see the damage they have caused you. If necessary, allow yourself to be emotional let out those tears that you've been holding on. Your partner can be touched to do the same so that you can get everything out in the open.

Take your time in deciding how to react

You don't have to come to a conclusion right away. Don't make any rash decisions you might regret further down the line. Assess the situation critically and take time to react. Before you can rebuild trust in someone after the disappointment, you need to evaluate if the relationship is one you want to salvage. You need to know if the request is coming from a sincere heart or another form of deceit. Try to know if the person is genuinely sorry for hurting you and ready to do everything perfectly from now on.

Forgive and move on

Forgive and move on when you are satisfied with your findings. You don't have to always treat them as a liar, but always be aware that someone who hurts you might take advantage of your good nature. Forget about your negative feelings, and don't allow suspicion to take over your life. But always be wary of those who have wronged you in the past.

Give and receive love. Try to accept an action that seems honest from your betrayer. When your betrayer tries to show affection, accept that the acts of affection are the real thing. You need to be willing to accept and love the person and you also need to accept the love that person gives you in return.

9 How to Deal With a Pathological Liar

Living with the pathological liar is difficult, even psychologically destructive. Trying to understand the mind and behavior of the pathological liar is something that requires a lot of wisdom, patience, intuition, and forbearance. The good news is that you can identify a pathological liar.

Learning how to protect yourself and learning the steps the liar takes will do you a lot of good. Most signs of pathological lying are still deeply embedded in a person's behavior. To spot a pathological liar, pay attention to their behavior and body language. Above all trust your instincts and discernment when dealing with a pathological liar.

Here are some signs that you're living with a pathological liar:

Pathological liars are good at studying people

Pathological liars are known to study the person they hope to take advantage of. They don't want their victim to know the truth; hence they try all means possible to divert people's attention away from their lies. In order to evade their victim and perfect their deceits, they usually study the person and examine what that person might or might not believe. Pathological liars have a good sense of which people will believe which lies, hence, they know how to appropriate their lies.

Pathological liars lack empathy

The pathological liar has no sense of empathy or consciousness. They seem to lack the ability to consider how the lying behavior may impact others. They don't care what you might feel in response to their lie. The pathological liar often shows no emotion when lying, which makes them believable. Ordinary liars are well aware of the consequences of lying to you. They feel guilty and will relax when you cease from asking them more questions but the pathological liars show no discomfort. Nothing seems to quite faze the pathological liar. The behavior is almost like an addiction.

Pathological liars exhibit strange behaviors

Reacting with anger is another technique used by the pathological liars. Studies suggest that pathological liars may become aggressive and angry when caught. Although no two pathological liars are the same, most of them will react aggressively when caught in a lie. When you try to have an open discussion about something that just isn't adding up, they can erupt in a rage. An ordinary liar will feel guilty, sad, or afraid that the other person would no longer accept them when caught, but a pathological liar will not. If someone seems to get angry in response to accusations of lying, you may be dealing with a pathological liar.

Body language

Many people assume pathological liars look sneaky and will refrain from making eye contact during conversation. This may be a wrong assumption; it may not be safe, jumping to conclusions about unusual body language. Some really experienced liars are good at giving you direct eye contact, and they will stare you in the eyes for as long as you talk. However, the thing to look for is eye contact that feels piercing-their pupils may dilate slightly, and they may also blink slowly.

Pathological Liars are manipulative

Pathological liars are good at manipulating people in a special way. They study people and know everything to say and do, they know what you want and don't want. They use emotional arousal to stimulate your intellect and distract you from the truth.

For example, in the case of police investigators, a seductive woman might try to stimulate her male prosecutors after being arrested. She can sit seductively, bend over while talking, or unbutton her shirt during interrogation to get the truth.

Lack of long-term relationships with others

An unstable relationship may indicate a pathological liar. Pathological liars tend to lack the ability to maintain long-term relationships. They don't have stable friendships or romantic relationships.

A pathological liar may also be estranged from the family.

Out of touch with reality

A pathological liar may have the tendency to exaggerate their ability and importance. They live in fallacy and are often disconnected from reality. A lot of times, they may believe parts of their lies themselves and become deluded about their abilities. They tell stories of victory even when it is obvious they are losing out. They find means of turning apparent defeat into victory by reconstructing the story. They will create whole histories that are fiction rather than just telling a little white lie. They don't seem to bother if the story is pessimistic or not, all that matters is their victory in the end. They talk a lot about the history of a personal heroism or how they were able to exploit other people easily, even when it didn't happen. When narrating a victory, they intentionally leave out the names of relevant people in order to take all the glory. They are good at using other's victories to appropriate accolades to themselves.

They are overly sensitive to criticism

They see criticism as a form of attack. Sometimes you don't need to show them directly that you disagree with their ideas, they detest criticism and will do all within their power to justify their position.

Dealing with Pathological Liars

Dealing with pathological liars takes tack and cleverness, because your emotional and physical health may be at risk. You need to master your emotional reaction to be able to explore various options. You may not be able to change the behavior of a liar, but you can change your feelings and reactions about them. Once you learn to regulate your emotions about a situation you begin to see a lot more options.

Change Begins with Awareness

Learn all you can about pathological lying and what motivates the behavior to better understand the person. Awareness helps us to deal with a liar without being upset. Awareness of the deeply entrenched social conditioning that influences a person to lie or behave in a certain way will help you review your expectations of the person. When you understand the rationale behind certain behavioral issues your expectations change. You will be able to deal with the situation in a way that isn't driven out of emotional reactions. Doing this does not mean that you learn to accommodate lying or condoning it, but instead, you gain a better understanding of why people compensate with lies the way they do. You will be able to use your emotional reaction appropriately to handle the situation in a positive way.

Listen to the person closely and watch for contradictions, which you can question in his narration. Stop him when he says something weird and ask him for the proof. Let them know that what was said is incorrect and confront him with evidence. Avoid open confrontation; remain calm while you make your point clear. Getting annoyed or blaming the person will not help the situation at this moment. Be gentle and supportive, yet firm when you confront them.

When you confront a pathological liar about their lies, their first reaction will most often be that of denial. They live in denial and do not accept the fact that they lie. It is up to their associates to convince them sympathetically that they have a problem which needs to be addressed immediately. Pathological liars can overcome the propensity to lie, but it takes willingness and, usually, therapy. Psychotherapy is identified as an effective treatment for people who suffer from this type of disorder. The treatment is typically a blend of psychotherapy, counseling, medication, role-plays, and practical assignments. It will take a lot of effort and steadfastness on your part to convince them and made them accept they have problems and start with the treatment.

Dealing with a person who lies compulsively is stressful especially if you have been giving chances and waiting for such a person to change but he remains adamant. The ultimate solution is to review your commitment to the relationship. If the person refuses to undertake treatment or even accept that he has a problem despite repeated attempts by friends and family. The relationship may be too toxic for you to handle, then you should consider staying away from the association.

10 The Benefits of Living Honestly

Honesty is the simplest thing you can practice in order to be happy, successful and fulfilled. Honesty is more than telling the truth always. It's about being real with yourself with respect to your relationship with others. It is about who you are, what you want and why you need to live your real life. Learning to be honest with yourself in everything is the more proactive approach to all situations in life. Honesty sharpens our perception and allows us to view things around us with transparency. Being honest with yourself is a great way to build trust, rise above life challenges, gain self-acceptance, and develop genuineness.

Here are some steps you can take to make you comfortable with honesty and live a happy and fulfilled life.

Accepting the consequences of lying

There is a price to pay for telling lies. Prepare to accept the consequences of the past lies. Since you want to create a change to betterment, accept your fault and admit on your weaknesses. Covering lies with lies will only make it harder for you to find a reasonable ground for honesty. Accepting the consequences honestly is crucial in transforming your life. Sometimes, it's better to own up to lies, and to past behaviors that gave you embarrassment, rather than trying to weave an elaborate web of lies to conceal the past. It can be beneficial and extremely healthy to come clean.

Once you take ownership of what you did in an honest and forthright way, you are on your way to get past the problem and move forward in life. This will help make self-honesty a little easier to incorporate into your daily living. According to Dustin Wax on Lifehack.org, "admitting your fault puts you one step closer to dealing with it, and can often be the first step towards a successful turn-around. At the least, though, it shows that you're someone with integrity and courage, even in the face of disastrous consequences."

Be open, be aware

How we view a situation is always influenced by our previous experiences, our upbringing, values, and some other factors. What might appear blue on the surface to you may appear black to others. This is probably due to the way the other person looks at the same set of facts or circumstances. Your own concept of truth may not be what someone else perceives as truth. Therefore, each individual has a worldview that is somewhat unique. One must understand this fact to be an honest person. In addition, you must respect the perspectives of others, and accept that truth is based upon your viewpoint and the degree to which you have access to the facts. Always try to see things from other person's point of view because the truth is more than what is right or wrong, but simply a perception of what is real. For instance, someone may see it as a failure not being able to accomplish a task within a specified time, while someone else may regard it as a learning experience and be less concerned by it or feel the need to justify the claim with lies.

Be honest with yourself

The truth is if you can't be honest with yourself, you will not be able, to be honest with others. Make a commitment to be honest with yourself, to regularly take time for self-evaluation. When you lie, the person you lie to the most is often yourself. It is important you make a regular appointment with yourself for personal appraisal. Be honest with yourself about what you say to your subconscious mind. Be responsible to tell yourself the truth about your behaviors, your feelings, your motivations, and your actions. Learn to be grateful for the great things about yourself, appreciate what you do well, and identify areas that need improvement.

Make a commitment

Honor your commitments, do what you have promised to do and always see your commitments through to the end. Be a man of your words. Commit yourself to live a life where you show openness through the goodness of character, integrity, and morality.

Stop comparing yourself to others.

Our desire to be like others can make us exaggerate and come up with deception to meet up for our inadequacies. You cannot overcome your inadequacies with lies but with constant skill development. People that always compare themselves with others tend to lose their actual visions and focus. They resort to what people say about them, instead of concentrating on the main purpose of their personal goal. If you stop being competitive with others and give yourself the worth you deserve, you won't feel the need to lie to make yourself acceptable. Speak truth to your heart without fear about whether or not it will make you look "bad." Most People admire honesty, even when the truth is painful.

Do not lie for others

Avoid situations in which you'll have to lie for others. The best you can do as a friend is to keep secret, not manipulating information.

Be careful with secret information such as the knowledge of a crime, a lie, or a harmful act against another. When someone tells you in confidence something that you know you cannot share with someone else, you should be prepared to offer your own disclaimer immediately to avoid entering into avoidable trouble.

Keeping this type of information puts you in a difficult position, especially when the whole thing comes open and the truth is revealed. Your integrity may be under doubt by the affected person when he gets to know that you knew all along.

Conclusion

Learning to be honest and seeking the truth with yourself is the more proactive approach to happy living. Honesty improves our vitality, engenders confidence and trust. It strengthens our willpower, represents us in the best way for others to emulate and endears us to friends and loved ones.

The opposite of honesty is lying. When you lie, you deceive yourself into believing what you're saying. You begin to live in fallacies. You lose your credibility, confuse yourself, confuse others, and put yourself in danger. Despite being easier than telling the truth, lying gets us nowhere in the end. It makes us be stagnant or much worse, take us backward. Learning to be honest and eliminating the need for lies can help to clean up your conscience and improve your relationships. Research evidence shows that speaking the truth improves both our physical and mental health. According to a study conducted by Notre Dame University, telling the truth when tempted to lie can significantly improve a person's mental and physical health.

About the Author

David has over 25 years professional experience working as a trainer, counselor, motivator, and administrator. He loves to help people change their lives and achieve their goals in life. David has written or edited a dozen of books where he shares practical techniques that anyone can use to make the desired changes in their lives.

Made in the USA
San Bernardino, CA
03 January 2019